Laurent F. Carrel

Messages from Melanie

365 Pearls of Wisdom and Hope from Afar

Laurent F. Carrel

Messages from Melanie

365 Pearls of Wisdom and Hope from Afar

May 16, 2016

To Anneli Diessen
with love, Laurent

Laurent F. Carrel
Messages from Melanie · 365 Pearls of Wisdom and Hope from Afar

This publication is based on the German title
"Trosttropfen der Hoffnung, 365 Engels-Botschaften und Ratschläge" by Bear CaLaFa
© tao.de · First Edition 2013

Published by tao.de, Goldbach 2, Bielefeld, www.tao.de, eMail: info@tao.de
© 2015 by tao.de, Bielefeld, Germany.

First Edition 2015

Author: Laurent F. Carrel
Photos and wooden sculptures: Laurent F. Carrel
Design: Kerstin Fiebig

ISBN Paperback: 978-3-95802-727-5
ISBN Hardcover: 978-3-95802-766-4
ISBN e-Book: 978-3-95802-767-1

Bibliographic information published by the Deutsche Nationalbibliothek.
The Deutsche Nationalbibliothek lists this publication in the Deutsche Nationabibliothek;
detailed bibliographic data are available in the Internet at http://dnb.d-nb.de.

Dedication

To the Messenger from Afar, my daughter Melanie.

In appreciation

To my wife Rebecca and my son Marc
for their assistance in translating the German into English.

To the trance medium Summer Bacon (channel for Dr. J.M. Peebles)
and the clairvoyant medium Jaimee McCabe
for their encouragement to travel the road of a spiritual warrior.

Foreword

All of us – whether we admit it to ourselves or not – struggle with Life in one way or another. How can we improve our lives and that of others? What is the meaning of our experiences? How can we heal from physical and emotional injury? What happens after death? If only we could understand what it is all about, perhaps through comforting messages and practical life counsel miraculously received from a knowledgeable Source … .

I am not that Source, only the transmitter of the messages that found their way onto paper *through* me, part of the almost 3000 which I have received and recorded since mid-2007. Sometime during each night, in a half-awake and sleep-heavy state, I scribble onto a waiting notepad, returning immediately afterwards to a deep sleep. The following morning, I am as surprised and delighted as you will be when I transcribe the nearly illegible words to reveal full sentences with profound meaning. The words that are written in *italic* were emphasized during the transmission, while a word in parentheses signals a double meaning. The use of "we" or "us" signifies the communicators in the Spirit World.

Exactly how the messages are transmitted is a mystery to me; some speak of the "nonlocal consciousness" to which we have access in many ways. If you have doubts about the origin of information in this book or you scoff at the process through which it arrives, you have my full understanding. With an academic and scientific background, as well as a keen interest in brain research, I would also prefer a rational explanation. However, over time it has become clear to me that it is less important whether I *believe* in this recurring contact with the spiritual realm than whether I *accept the reality and value* of the product so delivered.

There is no right or wrong way to interpret each message; the value is what you, the reader, give it. The meaning arises from your personal understanding. I hope you will agree with me that within this book there resides a power to console, to inspire, and to heal, as well as to make us smile.

I would like to offer another level of explanation about the origins of the Pearls of Wisdom and Hope from Afar, one that has its roots in my recurring bouts of sleeplessness and in the painful story of the premature death of our daughter Melanie over 35 years ago. After a long period of despondence about her loss, I was surprised one restless night that she appeared to me as a joyful, radiant spirit to accompany me into the world of sleep, then and every following night, thereby helping me as my "sleep angel" to instantly overcome my lifelong problem with insomnia. However, while the gift of a good night's sleep was already a miracle, another problem remained unresolved: I was still tormented by dreadful nightmares that made restful regeneration impossible. Encouraged by Melanie's presence, I appealed to the Spirit World for help. The very next night a spirit who had been a close companion during my childhood appeared in my dream, gave me his name and offered to help me overcome the nightmares. My guide was of the opinion that the frightening dreams were important for me and should not be suppressed. He would, however, assist Melanie to transmit a short message or piece of advice after every one. And that, dear reader, is how it started and how it continues to this day.

The current selection of messages was first published in 2013 in German under the pen name Bear CaLaFa with the title of "Trosttropfen der Hoffnung, 365 Engels-Botschaften und Ratschläge."

The Author's Journey

Dr. Laurent F. Carrel (*1945) lives in Switzerland with family ties to the USA. He completed law school and wrote his dissertation on U.S. environmental policy. After working many years as an attorney, strategy expert, crisis manager, university professor and author, he now runs a private practice in leadership coaching.

Since childhood, the author felt himself magically drawn to Nature's sources of energy where he could nourish ties to the spiritual world which continue to be strengthened and enriched today by profound life experiences. Additionally, he actively pursues an agenda of continuing education in spiritual growth where he has a particular interest in such subjects as mysticism, quantum consciousness, metaphysics, energy healing, yoga and meditation. While he has heretofore considered his spiritual experiences to be private, the author was gently encouraged by his contacts in the angelic realm - particularly by his daughter Melanie - to share the inspirational messages with the larger world and to drop his pen name Bear CaLaFa. The photos and wooden sculptures adorning this publication are the work of the author as well.

Foreword

January

1 We bring you light, we are the light:
the dark in you has no chance!

2 The power of prayer
is rooted in a deep promise –
to yourself.

3 Listen well!
Learn to pay attention to your inner voice –
we speak softly.
Pay heed to our advice,
take it to heart without hesitation,
we are with you.

4 What one has not experienced, one does not understand;
that is why your soul has undertaken a worldly experience.

5 Your longing for peace and simplicity
is a painful desire for closeness to us.

January

6 Sing your unique song with abandon –
sing it for yourself and then for everybody.
Carry the melody of your heart into the world.
We are ready: without you, our choir is condemned to silence.

7 To simplify is like to forgive: balsam.
It compels you to let go and brings healing.

8 Wonderful memories
are the salt in the tears of your life story –
they burn in the wounds of the unlived present.

9 The good you can do for each other
is without limits!

10 To approach people opens the world – and yourself:
practice it daily! In this way you give a gift to others to take with them
which later (without your knowledge) opens doors
and enriches their experience.

11　Your T-shirt carries the inscription "I am searching for (my) Self".
　　We have read it.
　　The answer lies on the path to yourself – and to us.

12　"Travel light": a motto for traveling and for living.

13　Everybody recounts his life stories, all tales from yesterday.
　　Let go of them and take what is – life, *your* life, now!

14　Before you lies a whole day.
　　Even if you fragment it into unrecognizable small pieces,
　　it remains a *whole day* that we place at your disposal.

15　You move in closed circles. Even when you change these,
　　you are either in or out, included or excluded, insider or outsider.
　　It is a game with boundaries that do not exist –
　　　　you are creating the illusion yourself.

16　Your true self flows in Being, in Light and in Eternity.
　　Only your worldly illusions of ego, power and possession are finite.
　　All that is important is timeless – love, hope, faith.

17 To help someone is a happiness booster!

18 At every moment, you can be both here and there –
in the presence of your ancestors
and of your descendants.

19 When your body rebels against the inundation of external stimuli
and closes the shutters, our advice is, "lay low" –
in a supine position you will discover new perspectives.

20 Create happiness!
Every moment is an opportunity to be the creator of your joy.

21 Roll out the red carpet for each new day
before you take your first step – today you write
your own script, tailor-made for yourself.

22 Because you race ahead at full speed,
you run aground again and again. And then?
Experienced captains remain calm:
the next high tide will free your grounded boat.

23 Good things will repeat themselves –
if you steer towards them.

24 So much in life is unclear, misunderstood, not settled.
Gauged by the required patience and energy,
„creating clarity" is a large part of life's program.

25 The ominous countdown to carry out your New Year's resolutions
can be interrupted at anytime – or you calmly continue
to count down and dare to start (into a new life).

26 With determination, you can quiet the mind
and invite the heart to sing! It vibrates with *your* music,
uniting you with the Universe.

January

27 When you look at your small world
through the lens of gratitude,
the corners of your mouth will turn
upward without fail.

28 Doctrines and dogmas are compiled in your inner dialogue,
by you and for you – you decide what has validity!

29 If you do not take your life dreams a small step closer
to realization without hesitation, they vanish unused –
like nightly dreams.

30 Light in the light – sunlight reflects on glistening white snow.
There are many ways to increase the intensity of light.
You too can shine more brightly: let your loving kindness radiate!

31 Savor the moment in which you are overwhelmed with gratitude.
Let your feelings flow freely and carry you
into the ocean of the All-Consciousness.

February

1 Your existence on earth is a precious vase
   which is at your disposal. What will you fill it with?
   What will you carry home in it?

2 To the question behind the question,
   there is always an answer behind the answer.

3 Dwarf fruit trees are pruned regularly to make it easier to pick their fruits.
How many people are not allowed to grow to their full potential
   because others want to take advantage of them?

4 Every page in the calendar is important;
   do not carelessly tear off any. Each one deserves
   your notation on the back: "I am thankful for…."

5 One can sleep too long in the morning and "miss the day"
   but gain it back nonetheless.
   Win depth instead of covering a lot of ground!

6 Your great dream to live as you wish,
    free of expectations and according to your vision of the future –
    becomes reality if you live it.

7 Children become your acid test: they check the authenticity of your feelings,
    the sincerity of your love, and your ability not to judge
    but to accept without prejudice – how *IT* is.

8 We always long to spend time with you
    but you often prefer to play with the distractions of your ego
    than to heed our wishes.
    At the end of the day, our claim on your time
    is based on your need – you just don't realize it yet.
    Thus, our question to you is, what conversation will we,
    with or without you, have anyway?

9 Dark, negative thoughts can be brightened with loving counter thoughts;
    you cannot forbid or ban them,
    but you can dissolve them in the light of love.

10 Is it a handrail, a cane or the arm of a companion
that prevents you from losing balance?
Don't forget that, above all, your inner bearing keeps you stable.

11 Find beauty in the desert:
beauty is manifested where you least expect it –
even in desolate circumstances and under dismal conditions.
It is the desert that makes an oasis a precious miracle.

12 Nature's reawakening from the dead of winter brings healing:
the blooming and greening is a promise to Life – and to you.
Mirror the beauty and wonder in you!

13 "Please wait!" On the telephone, at the counter, and at the check-in,
you are constantly being requested to "please wait".
Do you have the courage to ask: please wait for *me*?

14 Somersaults can knock the wind out of you –
is that the reason why you do them so rarely?

February

15 Preserve what is good in life, make your contribution,
protect and nurture the Light and put it where there is darkness.

16 You are frazzled, all your energy is sapped
by your busy-ness at the periphery – your thinking and doing.
Return to your center, gather your energy in your Being.

17 Consider your spiritual introspection as In-Sight,
to free yourself from being taken hostage by your guilt feelings.

18 Pray for someone in distress –
so many need your compassion.

19 Lessons following a standardized format are boring
because life's lessons do not follow a particular pattern.
The work you do on yourself is for you,
and yet for everyone.

20 Every day you make your own "weather forecast".
In contrast to the usual predictions, yours will always be accurate
because you can create your own sunny intervals – to clear up the darkness.

21 Can you lovingly caress the hair
of the exhausted I?

22 Have the courage and humility to collect yourself
in *one* drop and let it drip steadily
upon the stone of your (too) high expectations.

23 Your first impression remains –
but you can revise your opinion.
Look once again and give someone
a second chance!

24 Put your light *on* the table where it can shine –
without blinding others.

25 Whether in your dreams or in heaven –
somebody is waiting for you!

February

26 Often it is good thing to expect a lot from yourself and from others –
but remember to do it with a kind heart.

27 If you stay in your seat too long, you will miss your connection.
To change requires that you take your leave in good time.

28 Childlike affection – *the* scarcest commodity in the adult world.

29 Thankfulness has many faces:
all are gracious and come with a smile.

March

1 Do not search (in vain) for wine in the cellar –
the water is already on the table. How often do you (unsuccessfully)
chase after something supposedly better
when you can savor the simple things you already have?

2 Your perception = your reality:
how you tune in to it creates your tune.

3 Soak up the landscape, letting the scenery melt
and fuse into your being – then you are home and,
for a brief moment, in Divine Consciousness.

4 What is essential may be lost in disorderliness –
what is meaningful may meet the same fate in orderliness.

5 As fast as fog can obscure the view, a kind word and an offer of help
can illuminate new perspectives.

March

6 What can we celebrate today?
   What an astonishing question when an absolutely normal day is pending.
   Can you celebrate that it is only an ordinary day?

7 When you look into the mirror,
              your eyes reflect your Being instantly.
        The look in your eyes is the mirror of your soul.

8 You have too many choices.
     The process of elimination is your sedimentation tank –
         what remains are the priorities.

9 Not "lost and found" but "found and lost".
       How often do you find valuable truths
       that you discard carelessly or lose again … .
       Be mindful in the moment!

10 The mercy of the daily reset button: use your freedom to push it quickly –
        a fresh start can lead you in a completely new direction … .

11 Temporary setbacks boost your skill to open locks
with previously unknown combinations.

12 The seeds you plant with your thoughts will germinate
and you will harvest the fruits sooner or later, in one way or another … .

13 At night, your dreams bring to life
what you don't dare to dream during the day.
Could this be a hint to become more daring?

14 Breathe in and return home to yourself – breathe out and let go.
Use your breath to experience life at its fullest.
Your breath *is* your life. That's why we repeatedly challenge you:
breathe mindfully – live mindfully!

15 Why not have the courage to give a voice
to your inner child?

16 It is not important how many people love you,
but that you love yourself – so you can love others.

March

17 Put together a first-aid kit for your inner pain and suffering:
do it today ...

18 When you have crafted your own strait-jacket,
you know how to break the seams
and free yourself of it.

19 Time is one of the most loving and compassionate gifts
you can give someone, including yourself!

20 Things you do with joy and enthusiasm –
even if they are not expected or honored by anyone –
contribute to your happiness.
You and ultimately everyone will benefit from its fruits.

21 Perfection once was and will be again –
in between lies an enormous commitment to Life.

22 How can you handle your knowledge wisely? Use it to benefit everyone –
to share knowledge is as important as sharing bread.

23 You will not stop a steamroller by standing in front of it
but by letting it run out of steam.

24 If you look at the world from above, it becomes obvious:
everyone is on the move, those who are traveling as well as those
who aren't. On the Transit Life Journey, no one stands still.

25 During spring cleaning, windows are scrubbed to give a bright, clear view again,
dust and dirt are removed, unnecessary stuff is put into storage or disposed of,
and all the rooms are thoroughly aired out.
Do the same in the closets of your mind every day – morning and evening!

26 Your hand can also heal –
every hand can – don't hold it back!

March

27 Become Tefloned! Wrap yourself in a protective coating
which insulates you from sticky expectations,
inappropriate chores and obligations
which do not belong in your pan.

28 Dare to be who you are –
even if it means that you feel naked in public!

29 Why only dare to play a clown in secret?
There are many advantages to being a clown:
people have fun and you can tell the truth!
Dare to say what you think – dare to be daring!

30 Can you describe what your ideal day and your optimal daily routine look like?
It is the same in life – if you don't know what you really want,
you will not come close to it.

31 Everybody deserves a fair chance.
You decide how much value you give this statement –
and then you grant it to yourself too!

April

1 As you age, the constrictions loosen bit by bit.
Age will be your liberator and your ally. It will unburden you
from years long expectations of *what* and *how* you should be –
leaving you in freedom to be yourself.

2 Can you still let yourself be surprised by small wonders?
Like the first rays of sun on green foliage –
it is about your daily willingness
to see the grandeur in small things.

3 When you open your eyes, you will see multi-coloured variety,
diversity and multiplicity, opulence and richness in abundance everywhere –
divine gifts for yourself and others.

4 Jesus Christ was arrested, judged, and condemned –
practice being without judgment!

5 The demands placed on you are exorbitant
and what is expected from you is overwhelming.
Your hands are too small – place it all in *our* hands!

April

6 Is your thirst for serenity and (in)sight still not quenched?
Set forth on a pilgrimage deeply within *yourself*
to the place of silence and wisdom.

7 The love of details has its limits – especially when planning your life.
Given life's storms, your plans are no more than small vessels lit by hope;
the ships sink, but the hope continues to shine.

8 Even along the muddiest trail, flowers bloom.

9 The emptier you are on the *inside*, the more you cover up with superficial busy-ness.
It is worthwhile to pause and to explore your eternal connection to us.

10 At crossroads in your life, you are often burdened by the freedom to decide –
does it become a cross of doubt or a choice of hope and confidence?

11 Migrating birds return to where they hatched.
   Familiar places are sources of strength to which you can return home.

12 Every tear lightens your sorrow about the past;
wash the pain out – and heal!

13 Move out of the control range of other people
   into your own control room.

14 Your ailments are the speakers of your soul,
      an act of self-defense when you don't listen to it.

15 You see me on the cross, yet I am with you.
      You grieve, yet I have never forsaken you.
      You wait for me, yet I am with you.

16 In all honesty, what is the absolutely painless alternative
      to the aches and pains of aging??
Be realistic and thankful – for *everything*!
   Gratitude is the recognition that it is good how it is –
whatever IT is!

17 Dirt on your lens blurs the picture:
true not only for the camera –
your prejudices do the same.

18 In the school of life, you are both teacher and pupil.
What an opportunity! What a relief!

19 At the station platform, you have the choice to take *one* step
into the train, or not, thereby changing your world (and life).

20 After you breach a barrier, it can take a while
for a (your) path to open up.

21 Read the small print on your brake shoes:
RELEASE BRAKES AND LET IT ROLL!

22 Your inner child reaches for hammer, saw and paintbrush –
why not allow it?

23 Fire! Everyone calls for help.
Why not let the scrub brush burn away –
   the resultant clearing gives a better overview
and new (in)sights.

   24 Listen to the echo –
      it repeats many times over whatever you called out.
            Even your short, hardly noteworthy thoughts
      will return to the sender –
            and so you create your own world.

25 The meager portions you feed your soul
often seem inversely proportional to what you consume every day.
Be more generous in nourishing the vital force of your soul!

      26 Trapped in your head –
         what will it take for you to break through
            to your heart?

April

27 Trust Nature to restore your broken soul –
it is accustomed to cleaning up after storms and catastrophes.
Go listen to the trees, the bushes, the flowers, the animals and the birds.
What do they recount? And the other side, the wind and the water
which caused it all?

28 Kinks and ruptures in life leave spoors on your soul.
The journey back to read and understand them requires courage and strength.
The reward is the recognition of who you are!

29 What can you do today to contribute
to the healing and wellbeing of your body?
Start with giving much earned affection to your toes,
as they are your most loyal servants!

30 Watch out for clues:
what you need most will be given to you
at the right time!

May

1 At the core, you are untouchable –
your innermost self is fully protected.

2 Ding dong – every stroke
of the tower bell calls out to you:
just *be*…
be *just*…
just *be*.

3 A *medium* level of tension is good –
if the cords are overstrung or too loose,
your instrument will not sound full
and mellow.

4 The sun rises in the morning and sets in the evening –
but is always there, like your soul.
Its light is life – your life is light.

5 The truth is *in you* – how much room do you give it?

May

6 The beginning and end are not in your hands,
even when you end a life.

7 The ebb always follows the flood –
this makes so much sense!

8 Your adversaries will also get old and die defenseless.
What does that say to you?

9 Waking up – like the sun rise – is spectacular
and never ordinary: we take you in our arms
and give you back to life.

10 Animals sense when you are well-meaning –
by the way, people too.

11 The night has many faces –
   sanctuary in sleep is the most beautiful.

12 You are the beach for the waves of your children.
   Let their feelings wash up over you and recede.

13 You wait often and long for something –
   while it stands right behind you.

14 Deft and clever head work – clever and deft hand work.
   Why are they not equal?

15 Of the 10,000 things of everyday life, very few are truly useful and helpful.
   Cherish those that are!

16 You are so grateful that you are alive – we are so grateful that you are alive.
   You are mistaken when you fail to realize that we are also grateful
   that you live too!

17 Your humility and modesty
will find recognition in the right place!

18 The surprising is the absence of surprise.
The daily routine is *the* challenge.

19 Where in your so serious life is there something comical or funny to recount?
Lighten up – seriously, it is high time!

20 After a lousy day comes … a new day.
What small wonder can you marvel at today?
Perhaps, that you live?

21 You protect your hands from the cold with gloves –
do you have your soul-gloves with you too?

22 In case you have trouble with wonders –
        just try to explain what is at the origin of the healing process!

23 Wealth is what you already have – all wealth is within you.

24 The key is your hands:
        are they open or closed?
        Stretched out or pulled back?
        Folded or busy and healing?

25 Fog is the normal view of eternity –
        except for a few glimmers of hope.

26 When pauses define the beat – the rhythm is right.
    Mindfulness and rhythm go hand in hand.

May

27 Your restless drive to create is *the* chance
to be aware of timelessness.

28 Step out of the shadow – your own and others!
Be you with enthusiasm: serve life!

29 Even a monster backs off
when one feeds it lovingly.

30 Carry your burden as we carry you –
in peace and with strength.

31 The question is not how many trees you have
planted in life, but if they bore fruit.

June

1 You do not fully comprehend the essence of your spiritual guides.
This is no reason to be apprehensive about them.

2 You would like to be strong and victorious! And if you are the opposite –
weak and fighting your last stand but holding ground –
aren't you strong then too?

3 Tears are the curtain and the mirror
of your soul.

4 Your pain: breathe it in and burn it off
as healing energy … .

5 Your prayer: release me of my pain, anger, fear and constraints –
and set me free!

June

6 Everyday you are on the road to go home.
Yet, you are Home – all the time.

7 Closeness to God is closeness to oneself.

8 Small pleasures illuminate the soul.
This is why it is never too late to discover a new way
to do something loving for yourself.

9 Healing is a lifelong task.

10 To reflect every morning about the meaning of life
can bring meaning to your day – then live that meaning!

11 *How* you perceive the load determines
whether it is heavy or lightweight.

12 Mid-day = middle of the day,
mid-month = middle of the month,
mid-year = middle of the year.
Mid-life is all the time – no beginning, no end,
only middle in the Now.

13 No new day is like – everyday!

14 The closer to the goal you get, the more pressing the question:
is this the right one? The question answers itself
after you cross the finish line.

15 When something unexplainable by science makes so much sense,
which will you doubt – your senses or the science?

16 To see the glory and to experience it with all the senses –
this is grace.

June

17 All the tension you build up –
         in your body or outside –
you can tear down as well.

18 Between heaven and earth –
         you are so distant from both, yet so close.

19 Who abandons you if not you yourself?

20 Islands of smile sweeten and make your day.
         Smile ... .

21 All does not run smoothly –
         because *you* have edges!

22 Visit the graves of your fallen wishes and dreams: they died so young!
And yet, there are more budding everywhere ... .

23 The airwaves around the globe are filled
with invisible electronic communication –
nonetheless, you hardly know your neighbors.

24 What for some is a vital purpose in life
is for others an irrelevant fact:
this is part of the law of "separate realities".

25 A serious illness has toppled your overfilled life-jar,
spilling out all its contents so that you can fill it again:
not with a new, but with the *real* you – your true self!

26 When the Universe celebrates success –
are you a joint partner or a spectator?

June

27 The promise of accomplishment and success
seduces like the fruits in paradise. In hindsight,
the pleasure seldom meets the expectations.

28 A candle burns in unexpected places for you –
and awaits your hopeful wish.

29 One has to take leave from former companions
like a beaten path: decidedly, but in peace.

30 Bless your food before you consume it.
Bless your thoughts before you speak them.

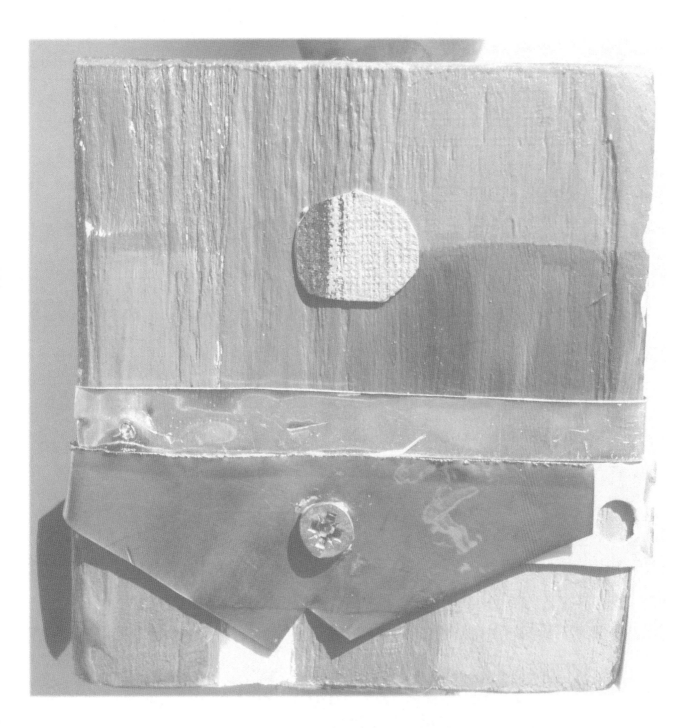

July

1 The first day is the last of the old – the last day is the first of the new:
creative energy helps to start again fresh, over and over again.

2 Friendship is like time, to be held with both hands – right now.

3 Mountain Trilogy
 a) Climb your steeply ascending life journey with courage –
        would you really want to descend already?
    b) On the mountaintop: savor the summit –
            practice the art of being in unity with All-Love.
  c) One cannot dwell on the summit forever.
       When you are "over the hump", the descent makes sense.

4 The decision to discharge dead weight becomes lifesaving
if one is flying in a balloon over a high power line.

July

5 Life is a huge treasure trove of experience –
why should everything be lost at the end?

6 Enticing vacation destinations are everywhere:
forgo these and travel instead – *to yourself*!

7 To tidy up creates space – and plenty of relief!

8 Forgive yourself for making detours in unknown territory.

9 The impossible vanishes –
like fear – if you tackle it.

10 How can you stay connected to the rhythm of the Universe?
Take up this simple challenge: pay attention to your breathing,
make yourself porous through it.

11 Why all the fuss about a dog in the church? Is it a church for Life?
To help an animal is like throwing a pebble into the water of eternity.

12 Life does not forgive half-heartedness –
least of all in old age.
If you only knew what you don't know,
you would pluck up your courage!

13 Forget that you were promised peace and quiet.
It is not that you are disturbed –
you let yourself be disturbed.

14 Choose your seat at the table carefully!
Where you sit down – there you sit!

15 The day must be saved early in the morning.

16 The blank sheet of paper before you is a challenge –
to also face emptiness.

July

17 To miss or lose a connection will change the journey –
often a good thing, so why worry?

18 When a critical illness knocks at your door, it opens by itself –
and all falls silent. Be attentive and change
what you are able to change – for everyone's sake!

19 The most harassing punch clock is you yourself. Have mercy!

20 You pay for the most expensive services in extravagant hotels
because you shy away from looking after yourself.

21 Younger talent takes over your job –
THE opportunity to devote yourself to *your themes.*

22 To be free is more than a dream;
it is a tough job, every day of your life.

23 Whether you look forward or back,
you cannot avoid looking inside of yourself.

24 Ostentatious uniforms are temporary symbols of power –
soon not understood without explanation when displayed in museums.
Magisterial might is short lived and fades –
the triumph of existence is timeless.

25 Thoughts rob you of your sleep, thoughts rock you to sleep –
you choose!

26 The time has come for you to put on an emotional armor
which protects you with Light and Energy
instead of with iron and steel.

27 (Re)conciliation starts in the head –
it is balsam for soul and body.

28 Illness and pain become your focus of attention, as well as an opening to Heaven:
even if you do not understand Heaven, it speaks to you.

29 When nothing helps, what will bring about healing?
Pray, dear disbeliever, pray. The hope for healing is anchored
in an unabated search into your Self.

30 In order to find your way back Home,
you have to know the vicinity of your heart
just as well as the geographical surroundings
of your dwelling.

31 Take to your breast only what you want to nurture and raise;
only that will nurture you too.

August

1 Learn from the longbow:
the bowstring is released, yet the arrow flies ... .

2 At times, break the door to the subconscious open with force –
even though an avalanche of pain bursts out.

3 To call a spade a spade is often the biggest challenge –
and *the* gate to resolution.

4 Blank spaces are a treasure trove of magical keys:
learn to read *between* the lines.

5 Why do you cross over dizzying suspension bridges
when the streambed runs dry?

August

6 We need to talk!
That is our invitation to you and everybody else.

7 All your unfulfilled dreams are stored in the lost and found bureau,
waiting to be retrieved by you. Reclaim your Self –
when and where possible.

8 It is impressive that a single person can generate concentrated energy
for a good cause. How about your inner "sacred fire"? How do you know
that it burns for a good cause? Does it consume your life energy
or does it warm you and others?

9 Only when you succeed in making order in your life
will you find your place.

10 You say, "He or she *is* somebody" and think everybody wants
"to *be* somebody". Nonetheless, you define yourself by what you *do*:
diligent busy-ness instead of luminous Be-ing.

11 Wiggle room does not open up by itself.
You have to force your entry, often in spite of yourself.

12 Restful quiet and a safe feeling while sleeping:
let it be night, let it be dark.
Dark? Don't be afraid, you are in good hands –
the Light is in you!

13 Thy name is All. Whoever whispers in the night, "Who are you?"
will receive the answer: "I am ALL, I am All That Is."

14 Daily we give you gifts to which you pay no heed –
what a pity, for they make your life richer.
Awareness and thankfulness can be learned.

15 When family and friends tease you, when life plays harmless hoaxes
and boisterous games with you: everybody means well – smile!

16 Pay attention to subtle distinctions:
which inner resistances need to be overcome
and which ones respected?

August

17 Light or dark? The color of the soul – not the skin –
is significant.

18 You are fully booked in the schedule of others.
Who rules your time, rules your life.
Do not forget: whatever you do, it is *your* time.
Why do *you* not take over the helm?

19 Pay attention: your many intentions, ideas and plans
of yesterday and tomorrow – implement them today!

20 Not only the authorities, but also *you* give yourself absurd orders.
Of what use are all these behavioral rules and instructions?
They compel you, again and again,
to become conscious of your freedom.

21 You feel like an outsider?
With us – and with yourself – you are always an insider.
We are all family; it is you who draw the circles
of inclusion and exclusion.

22 It is (not) astonishing how far you travel to find happiness,
although you can give it to yourself wherever you are.
Can you quite simply decide to be happy *now*?

23 God reveals Himself in your sleep – so that you wake up.

24 To renounce luxury is *the* ultimate luxury.

25 Do not take what is intended to be for everybody –
contribute to it instead!

26 The essentials get lost by overkill – simplify!
To simplify means to get to the essence of life.

27 Kiss your injury and your pain tenderly –
flowers of hope germinate in the healing wound.

28 It is relatively easy to elude the horns of a fighting bull –
you only have to rise above it.

29 When a celebrity dies, you make a huge fuss.
We give our full attention to everybody that joins us.

30 Rote learning, endless preparations and stress to pass examinations,
but life's tests are different! Is that comforting or unsettling?
For the true trials of life you need little – like courage or love.
The accumulated dead weight of knowledge is unnecessary.

31 How therapeutic to sweep things
that you have forgiven yourself and others under the rug of oblivion.
The thicker the rug, the deeper the sleep –
and the fresher the awakening.

September

1 When someone dies, you hold impressive funeral ceremonies —
every day of life deserves an equally joyful ceremony.

2 The light of God Consciousness is extinguished
by a whirlwind of thoughts —
only Pure Being shields the Light.

3 Life is often much simpler than your dreams.
You only have to wake up ... .

4 How can you lovingly accompany yourself into old age?
Lead yourself by a supportive arm —
you have never been so dependent on *yourself*.

5 The star-spangled sky —
a measure of the meaning(lessness)
of your preoccupations.

September

6 You are excluded from plenty of things;
not being included hurts, but you are part
of much, much more than you realize.

7 Kick the duck: even amiable creatures (like you)
need a little push from time to time!

8 It is high time to step out of your own shadow.

9 The achievement of *your* goals is meaningful and counts –
even when nobody notices!

10 You lock up young people in exam-cages in the name of education
and prevent them from discovering the true knowledge in themselves.

11 Is there anything more consoling then our promise:
we are waiting for you!

12 To feel bonded with EVERYTHING
is not only a feeling – it is the truth.

13 The only time you lose is in those instants
when you are not in the present moment.

14 When gratitude flows through you, you are truly with yourself and free.
Freedom at last!

15 Where you are is *your* place – fill it up!

16 Every day you watch birds fly –
nonetheless, you doubt that the Unseen carries you.

September

17 Not until the last drop of anger, rage or aggravation has melted away
are you free and healed!

18 To have stopped the rolling worst-case scenario train in the blink of an eye
and to send it headed in the opposite best-case scenario direction
is your greatest feat of today!

19 What you endure becomes your strength.

20 To take yourself (too) seriously –
can you see the humor in it and smile? How healing!

21 What speaks against your turning around
on the road of ambition that everyone is on
and choosing your own simpler and less ambitious path?
Especially since, in the end, all roads lead to the same destination … .

22 Your optimistic belief in the future is nourished
through a gushing pipeline of innovative ideas of the ALL-Consciousness,
waiting to be implemented by you.
Your creations are also ours, as well as the collective creations
of everybody: you are the co-creator!

23 If you willingly yield what is taken from you,
it will come back to you in one form or another.

24 Gratitude is not only the key to the hearts of other people,
but also the portal to yourself.

25 Youthful high spirits are like fresh morning dew, enjoy the sight.
The midday sun will dry up the pearls –
not your inpatient reprimands.

September

26 If you would like to cross over from the shady side of a valley
to the opposite sunny side, you first have to descend
and cross the even darker valley bottom
before you will ascend towards the sun – Go!

27 You can live separate realities simultaneously.
Schizophrenic people understand what you do not understand.

28 What you do, a thousand others do too.
That *you* do it makes it unique!

29 Four-leaf clovers grow along your path. Do you see them?
Do you pick them? How often good luck waits in vain!

30 The pain of separation is deep suffering –
face it with your ALL-Consciousness.

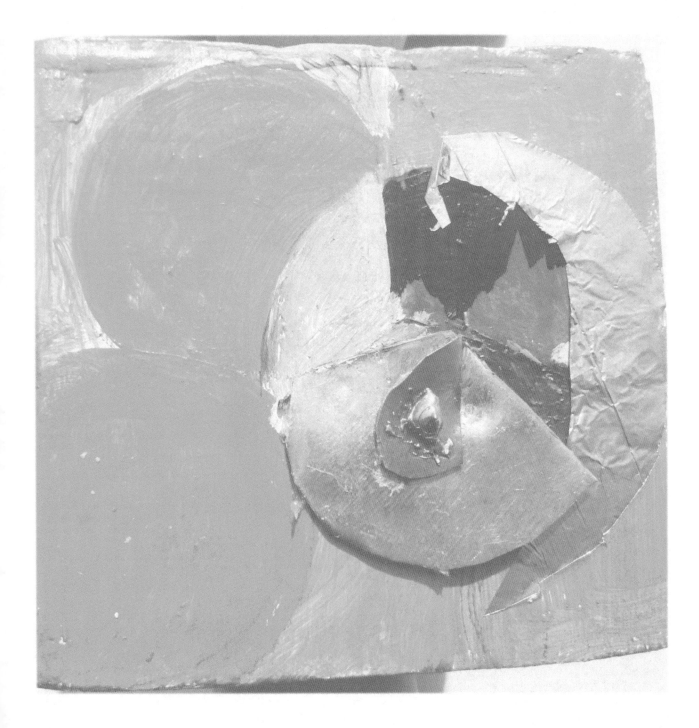

October

1 In the autumn of life, drop your colorful leaves and turn your attention inward –
so much strength is stored there.

2 Questions of the heart are also answered with the word "no".
Who am I – *not*? What with all my heart do I want – *not*?
What is the meaning of my life and existence – *not*?

3 It is astonishing what you pride yourself in knowing and understanding,
although your destiny (what God sends you) remains hidden
around the next corner, as does its meaning.
If you only knew what you do not know!

4 An intellectual sandstorm has walled off your heart with thoughts.
You can singlehandedly break down the wall only with a daily effort
to be in a state of Oneness – with lots of patience.

5 It is less the many souvenirs that burden you –
it is much more your *inner* burden that you drag along for years,
unable to either break away from or release.
In any case, what you really need on your journey you have with you –
(un)recognized?

October

6 Painful memories entangle you like blackberry brambles.
Relinquish your beloved garment to the thorns and move on –
look back only to forgive (yourself).

7 How you judge others is how you judge yourself;
what you give to others, you give to yourself;
love that you offer to others, you offer to yourself.

8 The key to the most precious part in you is in your hands exclusively.
No authority, absolutely nobody can (for whatever reason) lock you out –
other than you yourself!

9 In the midst of uncertainty, the echo of every spoken word is magnified.
That is why in these moments, you and everybody else need words of comfort
and hope.

10 Even if your hands hold an empty cup –
they are not empty.

11 The bus has departed, as has the train;
   likewise, the airplane took off without you,
everybody else was on board.
   Be happy to have missed all the connections –
but to have made the *connection to yourself*.

12 You must free yourself to free others;
   you have to wound yourself and others in order to heal yourself and others;
   you have to fight in order to learn to make peace.

13 When the Truth enters your life,
   no doubts remain *"whether the Light is or is not"*.
   The Divine Love shines brightly like the sun,
all earlier priorities recede into the shade.

14 With every loving gesture you give yourself and others,
      you allow the Divine Light of God to shine.
   You become the love you are seeking.

15 Even among the infinite multitude of waves in the ocean,
         you are a unique white cap –
   and simultaneously remain part of the Whole.

16 As you relinquish position to the next generation of talent
      and cede the stage to them, your ego-shadow dissipates in the light
   which shines back to you.

October

17 The resolution of interpersonal problems often lies in the small plug adaptor which connects and enables energy to flow and become light. Your angels willingly help you to find the adaptor – or to be it yourself.

18 Your spiritual vision ought to be simple, clear and effective. For example: less irritation and annoyance, more patience and love towards yourself and others.

19 You are not in the shelter of your house – the shelter is in you!

20 The reconciliation with yourself and others starts in the heart. Then, step by step, it has to conquer the head.

21 "Spirituality" is a stilted word. Translated into daily practice, it means nothing else than to give a gift of God's love to yourself and others and to live it as a daily experience.

22 Everything you call "your possession" is given to you –
like leaves to a tree. They serve it, they become colorful in the fall
and drop off. At the end, you stand there too – as you are!

23 You can choose between layers of consciousness
and layers of reality.

24 Swallows and starlings migrate to their wintering grounds
as the days grow shorter, their flight heralding the oncoming autumn (of life).
You are also part of the orderly cycle.
You will (live to) see the next spring, wherever!

25 Master your inner dialogue
and you master your destiny!

26 Your constant search for things
that are close to your heart and that you cannot find
has a deeper meaning:
not to give up the search!

27 Even if you are having piecemeal experiences of God,
you are unable to connect the dots in order to see the entire Big Picture.
It is granted to a few – although everybody is part of it!

28 Does it concern you if in old age the external demand for you
and your services is dwindling? It is an unmistakable sign of a new yearning:
the I needs you! You need yourself now.

29 No sound can be elicited from the instrument,
it remains silent, it was misused for too long a time –
it is no different with human beings.

30 Once again, you are spared from a grave accident
at the last minute. That you do not believe in guardian angels
does not mean that they do not exist.

31 What Nature reveals in one wink of an eye
is more knowledge than you ever learned in school.

November

1 The first snow blankets the scarred earth –
the self-healing forces of Nature need rest
in order to unfold. That's what you need too.

2 You succumb to the illusion that it is crucial
on which side of a locked door you stand. If you abandon the ego-world,
you will stand on both sides – the passage way is open.

3 The ruptures in your life story are often noticeable on your (in)visible scars.
They serve to remind you not of the wounds
but of the lessons you learned.

4 You struggle valiantly to keep the balls from rolling off the table,
but the table slopes and life is ever changing.
Instead of conducting this futile battle, wouldn't it be better – here and there –
to pick up a ball from the ground and put it back on the table?

5 You are horrified to speak publicly and without written notes.
If you speak from your heart, you do not need any script.

November

6 Your mantra is simple and does not require a guru:
breathe God in, breathe love out –
with love to you, to everyone and to ALL.

7 Your everyday life – no wonder you are stressed and burned out!
If you would play the game of life according to *your own* rules of love,
it will bring you joy and fun.

8 Freedom is to set sail into the day and let the wind decide
whereabouts it carries you.

9 The challenges in life are enormous – that is why you are here.
The challenge to love is the greatest;
to understand this and to live it
is an entire lifework!

10 No matter what people tell you, *your* free will decides:
the real authority is your heart in God!

11 After an injury, our healing power is at work day and night,
without interruption. For a complete recovery,
we rely upon your healing thoughts – likewise around-the-clock.

12 Although the reserved seats promise protection from the rain,
they are often shaded, while the unsheltered standing room
enjoys the warm sun.

13 A natural gas pipeline supplies different houses.
In one, a celebrity chef is at work; in another, the stove is little used –
at best water is boiled. We endow you with life, energy and talent –
whether and how you use it becomes the question and task in *your* house.

14 While there are many ways to embellish or conceal flaws in your appearance
as you age, the glow from your heart remains flawlessly pure and true.

15 Giving away things does not mean you cannot use them any longer,
but that you realize other people can use them better.

16 There is no bigger challenge then to love.
If you rise to the test, your life will be altered –
forever and for better.

November

17 You dream of being a hero.
Everybody wants to be one! And yet, you are all heroes –
just for being!

18 Goodness is light – it shines in the eyes!

19 In winter, the plankton turns into sediment
and the lake becomes transparent all the way to the bottom.
How cold does it have to become *in you*?
Must you have accidents and illness to cool down
your hyperactivity machine to gain such a depth of clarity?

20 If somebody already tosses your time and goal plan out the window
in the early morning, does this mean – not more and not less –
that you simply adopt *his* agenda instead? (Or that your plan was made
of sand instead of weighty rocks?)

21 He has the highest position, he wears flashing stars on his uniform
and he wants to be recognized and acclaimed by you.
Bestow your esteem on those who live in the Light –
they have stars from above to guide them.

22 You are like a life-prospector,
   always searching for the "big strike" —
but finding small veins
   that make sure you stay a prospector.

23 Even when all the social and medical safety nets have failed you,
you are still held by God's love.

24 Wherever you are not,
   things are changing as much as where you are;
      you only realize it when you return.
      That everything stays the same may be your wish,
      that everything changes may be your aspiration!

25 When you ask someone for a small favor
but receive multiple favors instead, do not ask why —
   just double your gratitude.

26 Learn for the next lesson —
   learn about "forward learning".

November

27 Plenty of things were here before you were born
and they will still be here long after you are gone.
Think about that the next time you throw a stone
mindlessly into a river.

28 Efforts to embellish your results
in order to gain external approval will reflect like in a concave mirror.
In the focal point shines the truth: value is found within!

29 Inventions in a dream, even if these are never realized,
are evidence of wisdom outside of the brain.

30 Create free space for yourself to rest and recuperate –
constricted, no healing can flourish.
Often you need not only to loosen a stranglehold
but also to cut through it: the results will be spectacular.

December

1 How can you make everyone understand
that from now on you celebrate your birthday every day?

2 Farewell as a new beginning – what a platitude.
If this is so trivial, why not put it into practice everyday?

3 Candlelight makes visible what is always there: the light of God.
Take the Light, carry it in you, surround yourself with Light,
pass it on … .

4 The crucial difference lies not in what you do but in who you are.
Reduce the time you squander on planning and organizing your activities:
your Being leads you into the Light.

5 Whenever you stride from north to south or from east to west,
you cross the vertical link of the opposite poles of zenith and nadir –
midway you find *your* center.

December

6 Let yourself be surprised – even by a Santa in disguise
with an obviously fake beard. Play the game and stay open,
embrace well-meant surprises like small wonders.

7 How you nourish others becomes your own nourishment.

8 Every decision is linked to a chosen point in time.
Every (chosen) point in time is linked with the hologram
of the greater whole – so is the tenor of each decision.

9 Follow your star, rescue your dream
(wherever – whenever).

10 We give you dreams and experience; we give you energy and information.
They are real and always will be. Whether you make use of them, let them pass
or even push them away is your choice – and becomes *your* reality.

11 The direct, no-frills approach may work, but it is often joyless.
The curlicues of life can be charming and pleasurable.

12 So many voices in the ether would like to communicate with you
but you do not understand them, they are not your frequency, they sound foreign.
Do you at least understand your own inner voice,
does it speak your own language?

13 You deal violently with each other in order to win
because you do not understand that to conquer love
is the ultimate victory.

14 You do not understand your dreams as you do not understand your life.
This should not prevent you from sleeping soundly and living well.

15 Did you think it was only a coincidence
when help suddenly appeared at your wayside and took over your burden?
This is evidence of our help which is always waiting there for you.

16 Images which arise during contemplation
are images in you which aspire to come to life.

December

17 Our information for you comes from afar – very far.
On their way to you, even the thickest walls cannot stop them.

18 The energy we send to you is love.
Keep your hands and your heart open.
What you receive you can pass on,
what heals you, heals others.

19 To step aside means to let *IT* happen without judgment
and without expectations. Only then can *IT* flow and heal.

20 Whatever you imagine is a (your) reality.
A (your) vision becomes reality due to your imagination:
all wonders follow this path.

21 The thirstier you are, the more delicious the pure water –
it's the same with divine love.

22 Your wishes, like your feathered friends, land silently on the soft snow – freezing but searching hopefully for food.

23 Shelter from danger and uncertainty? Many times a crib in a barn suffices.

24 For you, Christmas is a treasure chest of memories; for us, it is the recurring birth of Hope.

25 Christmas signifies light – a lit tree and candles everywhere. Look at each other – *you* are the Light.

26 To flee can be a blessing.

December

27 Energy flows from your heart
and reconnects with the Universe
from where it originates.

28 In the middle of the night, a question arises
needing a clear answer: what is the purpose of your *doing*?
In the daylight your *being* can answer.

29 With the rising and falling of the tide of life, you learn to let go
and to make contact, to separate and to bond, to give and to take,
all in due time. Your soul knows:
"There is plenty of time – time is on your side."

30 When you cup your hands in gratitude,
divine bliss flows and fills your core –
for a moment you taste timeless eternity.

31 The years pass by: what is lost is found in you,
lying close to your heart.